A

Seared Conscience

Charles G. Finney

❦

Contents

The Bible speaks of a seared conscience in 1 Timothy 4:2 . . .

A Seared Conscience

I. What Conscience Is Not:

1. It is not the mere knowledge of right and wrong.
2. It is not the mere knowledge of whether we do or do not, have or have not done, or been, or said, or felt right or wrong.

II. What Conscience Is:

1. Conscience may be regarded, either as a power or as an act of the mind. In the former case, it is that power of the mind that affirms and enforces moral obligation, and that pronounces upon the desert of obedience or of disobedience. Conscience is not a legislator that makes law, but a judge that convicts of guilt, passes sentence, in respect to the past, and decrees and enforces moral obligation to obey law, in regard to the future. Conscience, as a judge, smiles upon obedience, and frowns upon disobedience.

As an act of the mind, conscience is an affirmation or testifying state of the reason, in respect—

(1.) To the agreement or disagreement of the will with the law of God.

(2.) With respect to the moral character of this agreement or disagreement of the will with the law of God.

(3.) With respect to the good or ill desert of this agreement or disagreement.

(4.) With respect to our moral obligation to obey in future. In short, it is the conscious affirmation or felt testimony of the reason upon these points. It seems sometimes to be used in the Bible as including that state of the sensibility, compunction, and distress on the one hand, or of conscious peace and happiness on the other, that is naturally connected with the emphatic affirmations of reason. The Bible is not given in philosophical language; but for the most part in popular language. And I am persuaded, that the popular understanding of the term conscience often, if not always, includes that state of the sensibility which we call remorse, or approbation. I do not, in this definition, intend to speak in strictly scientific language; and what I have said is sufficiently accurate for the purpose of possessing the minds of those who do not study metaphysics, of what is intended by conscience.

III. What Is Intended *by* a Seared Conscience:

1. It is the refusal or neglect of the reason, or that power of the mind, whatever you may please to call it, which makes the affirmations of which I have just spoken, to enter into judgment, and make these emphatic representations of moral obligation or of guilt.

2. A man may know his duty, without feeling impelled by an emphatic affirmation of moral obligation to do it.

3. He may know that he is or has been wrong, without the consciousness of being arraigned, convicted of guilt, and condemned. This state of mind clearly indicates a seared conscience.

4. The figurative language of the text implies, a state of insensibility to moral obligation, and of ill desert for moral delinquency.

5. A seared conscience may be general or particular; that is, the mind may become generally insensible to moral obligation and the ill desert of sin; or this insensibility may be confined to particular sins.

IV. What Are Evidences *of* a Seared Conscience:

1. A general apathy on moral subjects, is conclusive evidence of a generally seared conscience, and is a most guilty and alarming state of mind.

2. Apathy on particular moral subjects, is an evidence of a seared conscience, in respect to those particular subjects.

3. When questions that concern our own well-being, or the well-being of others, are not regarded and treated as moral questions. For example—when the Abolition of Slavery, Temperance, Moral Reform, Politics, Business Principles, Physiological and Dietetic Reform—when these, I say, are not treated as moral questions, and as imposing moral obligation, the conscience must be in a seared state.

4. When questions that respect our own usefulness, or the usefulness of others, are not treated as moral questions, it is because the conscience is seared with a hot iron.

5. When the choice of a profession, companion for life, or anything else, that must increase or diminish, or in any way have a bearing upon the moral influence we are to exert upon the world, fails to be regarded and treated as a moral question, of serious and deeply solemn import, and as imposing moral obligation of awful magnitude, conscience must be seared with a hot iron.

6. When you can neglect to inform yourselves, on such subjects, without a sense of guilt; especially when the means of information are within your reach; and still more especially, if the subject be presented to your consideration, if, under such circumstances, you can remain quiet in ignorance, in respect to any question of usefulness or duty, without a deep sense of guilt, it brings out the demonstration that your conscience is seared with a hot iron.

7. When you can neglect any known duty without the bitterness of remorse, your conscience is seared with a hot iron.

8. When you can trifle with your health; go out in the snow or wet, with thin shoes and hose, or in any way inappropriately clothed, unless you are under the necessity of doing so, your conscience must be seared with a hot iron. When you can neglect to ventilate your room, see that you have not too little or too much fire—in short, when you can in any way trifle with your health, that precious gift of God, without conviction of guilt, your conscience is alarmingly seared.

9. When you can trifle with your time; spend it in reading plays, and novels, mere slang in newspapers, or in any other way, squander an hour or a moment of your precious time, without compunction, your conscience is already seared.

10. When you can hinder others and trifle with their precious time, without remorse, your conscience is seared. Suppose you have an appointment to meet others on business, and are behind your time, and hinder them; what an evil is this. If you can be guilty of it without remorse, your conscience is seared as with a hot iron. If you have boarders, and do not prepare their meals punctually, but hinder them by not having their meals in readiness at the specified moment; you have

done them and the cause of God an injury. And if you do not feel condemned for this, it is because your conscience is seared.

11. If you do not feel condemned for coming late to meeting, and disturbing the worship of God's house, it is because your conscience is seared with a hot iron. Especially is this true, if you are a minister, and are in the habit of being behind your time.

12. If you can stand and talk with and hinder a man while at work, or in any way cause him to spend a moment's time in vain, without remorse, it is an evidence that your conscience is seared.

13. When you can squander your possessions in any way, and consume them upon your lusts, without remorse, your conscience is seared as with a hot iron. If you can spend God's money for tobacco, or any unnecessary and unwholesome articles of luxury or dress, without deep compunction, it shows conclusively that your conscience, upon those subjects, is seared with a hot iron.

14. When you do not feel that you are stewards, and absolutely and practically regard yourselves in this light, in respect to all the possessions you have, it is because your conscience is seared with a hot iron.

15. When you can in any way disregard the rights of others, in things never so trifling, it indicates a seared conscience.

16. When you can neglect to pay your honest debts, or when you can consider yourself as not to blame for being in debt, especially when your debts were not contracted under the pressure of an absolute necessity, it is because your conscience is seared with a hot iron.

17. When you can lay a stumbling block before a brother, without compunction or remorse; when you can indulge in any course of life that has a tendency to mislead him—when you can unnecessarily try his temper, say or do anything that has a tendency to lead him into sin, it indicates a seared conscience.

18. When you can suffer difficulties between yourselves and others to remain unsettled, without using every Christian means to adjust them, it proves that your conscience is seared as with a hot iron.

19. When you can be in the habit of borrowing and using your neighbor's tools, without perceiving and feeling the injurious tendency of such conduct, and without realizing the pernicious principle on which such a practice turns, it is because you have a seared conscience. Many persons act as if they supposed that conscience had to do with but one

side of this question—that it is the lender exclusively, and not the borrower, who is to look to his conscience, and see that he does not violate the principles of benevolence. But let us look at the principle contained in this. If you borrow money of a man, you expect to pay him interest, or at least to restore the same amount you borrow; but if you borrow a man's coat or tools, that are injured by wearing, it is the lender and not the borrower, that has to pay the interest, and often a very high rate of interest too. Many a man has lost his tools and paid at the rate of twenty-five per cent for the privilege of lending them. Now suppose a man has a hundred dollars in money. Money is scarce, and a hundred men desire to borrow it, everyone in his turn. And now suppose each one should wear a dollar out of it. The man's hundred dollars are soon used up. But suppose a man should come to you and ask you to lend him money and insist upon it that you should pay him interest, instead of his paying you interest, and you should say, "Why, I never heard of such a request! Do you ask me to lend you money and pay you interest besides?" Now any man would be ashamed, and would have reason to be ashamed, to make such a request; and his naked selfishness would in such a case be most manifest to everyone. And who would think of accusing the lender of selfishness, in such a case, if he should refuse to let his money go for nothing, pay interest besides, and finally take the trouble to go after it. And yet this involves precisely the same principle upon which many persons conduct, in the neighborhoods where they live, in continually borrowing and using up their neighbors' tools, and perhaps compelling them to go after them, and that too without compunction or remorse. Nay, so far are they from feeling compunction or remorse, and perceiving that they are actuated by the most unpardonable selfishness, that they would complain, and suppose themselves to have a right to complain of the selfishness of a neighbor who should refuse to indulge them in acting upon such principles.

By this I do not mean to say, or intimate, that it is not proper and a duty, in certain cases, for neighbors to borrow and use each other's tools. But this I do say, that the practice as practiced, is unjustifiable. Borrowing should not be resorted to, except in cases where a man might, without any cause for blushing, ask a man to lend him money, not only without interest, but also ask him to pay interest.

20. When you can neglect secret prayer, without feeling condemned, and a great sense of guilt resting upon you, it is because you have a seared conscience.

21. The same is true when you can perform secret prayer slightly, with little or no feeling, faith, or earnestness.

22. The same is true, when you can indulge wandering thoughts, and use words in prayer without scarcely knowing what you say, and all this without deep compunction and remorse. This state of mind is a certain indication of a seared conscience.

23. When any duty is urged upon you, without your feeling the force of moral obligation to perform it—when truth and argument do not take hold of your mind, and deeply impress you with a sense of responsibility—and when, in such a case, you do not feel the impressive affirmations of conscience, impelling you to the discharge of duty, it indicates a seared conscience.

24. When you can satisfy yourselves with the outward performance of duty, while your heart is not right—when you can satisfy yourselves with the mere form of religion and duty, while your heart is not deeply engaged in it, and this without a deep sense of guilt, it indicates a seared conscience.

25. When you can neglect the means of grace, or attend upon them carelessly, in a prayerless, heartless manner—when you can indulge wandering thoughts under preaching or in reading your Bible; when you can go to and return from meeting, without earnest prayer, that the word may be blessed to you—when you can hear and soon forget what you hear, without solemnly laying it to heart, with a fixed purpose of entire obedience—when these things can be without deep compunction, it is because your conscience is seared with a hot iron.

26. When you can satisfy yourself with anything, as a performance of duty, while you are not actuated by love, without compunction, it is because your conscience is seared, and become very superficial in its affirmations.

27. When light upon any subject does not cause your conscience to enter into judgment, strongly affirm moral obligation, and pronounce its sentence upon you, if you neglect your duty, it is because your conscience is seared with a hot iron.

28. When evidence makes but little impression upon you—when it does but little good to reason with you—when light, truth, argument, seem to pass over your mind, without lodging in it—when you are not convicted and converted, by a reasonable degree of evidence—when you do not feel yourself shut up to the necessity of yielding to a preponderance of evidence, or falling under deep condemnation, it is because your conscience is seared.

29. When the discussion of any important practical question can be postponed, and give place to matters of less importance—when you can lay up such a question for future consideration, and go on in courses that are at least questionable, merely designing at some future time to examine and settle the question—when this can be done without a deep sense of guilt, it shows that the conscience is seared with a hot iron.

30. When any form of selfishness can be indulged, without compunction, it is because you have a seared conscience.

31. When you can transact business upon selfish principles, take advantages in business, that shall put money in your own pocket at the expense of another—when you can enrich yourself by any employment, without regarding the interest of those with whom you deal, as you do your own, your conscience is seared with a hot iron.

32. When you can complain of a want of conviction of sin, this is evidence of a seared conscience.

33. When you can neglect to make confession of your sins to those who have been injured by them, and thus persist in your injustice and wickedness, without remorse, your conscience is seared with a hot iron.

34. When you can make excuses for not confessing—when you do not feel impelled by a sense of duty to make full confession—when you can satisfy yourself with a heartless, constrained, or partial confession—when you can be satisfied with a private confession, when it ought to be public—when you can be satisfied with confession, without repentance—your conscience is seared with a hot iron.

35. When you can neglect to make restitution, to the extent of your ability—when you can retain in your possession that which in equity belongs to another—in short, when you can hold on to possessions that were obtained by a violation of the great law that requires you to love your neighbor as yourself—when you can hold on to them, without

restoring them to their rightful owners, when it is in your power, it is a demonstration of a seared conscience.

36. When you have no sense of moral obligation in respect to those habits of life, that have an influence upon your brethren, your family, the community in which you dwell, and upon the world at large, it is because your conscience is seared. For example—if you have no conscience on the subject of retiring to rest in due season, and rising in the morning also at such an hour as best consists with health—if you can habituate or allow yourself, on any occasion, without necessity, to sit up late at night and rise late in the morning—if you can have no system in this respect, no principle, no conscience about it—if these things are left without consideration or reflection, to the neglect and injury of your own health, the injury of your family, and of course to the injury of the Church and the world, your conscience must be seared with a hot iron. If you have no conscience in respect to observing these things, for your family's sake; and if you do not require them and all under your control to have system, principle and conscience upon these subjects, from which they will no more depart without imperative necessity than they would go without their necessary food, it is because your conscience is seared.

37. When you have no conscience in regard to your modes of dress— if you can compress your chest with tight lacing, or in any other way expose your health, for the sake of personal appearance, without compunction of conscience, it is because it is seared with a hot iron.

38. When you can wear ornamental dress, consult appearance rather than utility, in your dress and equipage; can have regard to the fashion, rather than to health, utility, or Christian economy, without compunction, your conscience is seared.

39. When you can neglect cleanliness, in respect to your person, your dress, your house, or your furniture, your conscience is seared.

40. When you can neglect to attend to things in their proper season, or only transact your business in a careless and slovenly manner—when you can leave your tools where you use them, without putting them in their place—when you can leave them exposed to the weather, leave your barn doors open, and things around you in a state of confusion and disorder—when you can waste anything—in short, whenever you can neglect to attend to every duty that belongs to you, at the right time, in the right manner, and in all respects as it ought to be attended to,

without feeling condemned for this neglect, it is because your conscience is seared with a hot iron.

41. Whenever you can, through any neglect or carelessness, break anything, injure the tools, furniture, or anything else with which you are entrusted, whether it belongs to yourself or anyone else, without compunction, your conscience is seared.

42. When you can neglect to ventilate your rooms, air your beds and clothing—neglect to exercise, labor, or rest, or to attend to anything else that your health and highest usefulness demand, without a sense of guilt and condemnation, your conscience is seared.

43. When you can neglect to support the institutions of the gospel, to the extent of your ability, to pay your minister's salary, to aid in the support of the expenses of the church—when you can see the house of God lie waste, the doors and windows out of repair, the house in a filthy state, the stoves out of order, and things at loose ends—when you can suffer these things to be, without deep compunction of conscience, your conscience is seared with a hot iron; and when a church is in a state to suffer such things, without deep remorse and self-condemnation, the conscience of the church is seared.

44. But to notice again personal habits, if you have no system, no conscience, no principles in respect to the hours of eating and drinking, but allow yourselves to consult convenience rather than physiological law, taking your meals at one time many hours apart, and at other times within three or four hours of each other, thus recklessly violating the laws of God established in your own constitution, your conscience is seared.

45. If you have no conscience in respect to the kinds of food and clothing, with which you attempt to supply the physiological wants of your system, if you can neglect to inform yourself in respect to what your habits ought to be in order to secure your highest health and usefulness, if you can make your depraved appetites the guide and measure of indulgence, without deep remorse, it is because your conscience is seared with a hot iron.

46. When you can waste God's money in administering to your lusts, when you can buy tobacco, tea, coffee, and such like fashionable but pernicious articles without deep compunction and remorse, your conscience is seared with a hot iron.

47. When you can say you have no conscience on these subjects, when you can give countenance to these practices, and to the use of these articles at home or abroad, when you can use them yourselves, or furnish them for your friends, and thus countenance practices by which the Church is expending a hundred or a thousand times as much in poisons, and in the gratification of depraved artificial appetites, as it is for building up the cause of Christ and saving deathless souls from hell, when you can hear the wail of hundreds of millions of immortal beings coming upon every wind of heaven and crying out for the bread of life, and still have no conscience on the subject of the use of these pernicious articles, by which the Church is poisoned, and the heathen robbed of the everlasting gospel of the blessed God—if you have no conscience on such subjects as these, it is because your conscience is seared with a hot iron.

48. When you can see the Church indulging in such things and not reprove them, at home or abroad, especially by the impressive lesson of your own example, you must be extremely hardened, and your conscience seared as with a hot iron.

49. When you can neglect to scrutinize your motives of action, and go on day after day without self-examination in this respect, when you can neglect to exercise a godly jealousy over yourself, without remorse, your conscience is seared.

50. When you can speak evil of a neighbor, when you can publish his real or supposed faults without necessity, and do this without remorse, your conscience is seared.

51. When you can suffer sin upon a brother without faithfully reproving him and yet not feel compunction of conscience, it is because it is seared.

52. When you can feel contempt for the person or talents of any one without deep remorse, it is because your conscience is seared.

53. When you can think of sin without horror, something as they would feel at such a thought in heaven, it is because your conscience is seared. How think you an angel would feel if the thought should come over his mind—to-day I shall sin against God? How would a saint in heaven feel under the same impression? Why, it would come over all heaven like the shock of an earthquake. They would all stand aghast and grow pale, would hang up their harps, and wail out with pain at the thought that one of their inhabitants should sin against God. Now what

state of mind must that be when you can expect to sin without the deepest horror, without feeling a chill come over you and your blood almost coagulate in your veins. What, sin against God! Why, if the thought does not shock and agonize you, if the expectation that you shall sin does not seem even more terrible to you than death, where is your conscience—in what state of mind are you? Have you any sympathy with heaven? No, indeed. And perhaps I might and ought to say that if you can think of sinning without the most excruciating agony, you are even more callous than they are in hell.

V. How *the* Conscience Becomes Seared:

1. The conscience becomes seared by the will resisting the affirmations of reason. The conscience is now generally supposed to be a function of the reason. Whether it is regarded in this light or not, it is certain that it becomes seared when the will opposes itself and continues opposed to the decisions of the reason.

2. Especially does the conscience become seared, when the will persists in courses directly denounced or condemned by the conscience. In such cases the conscience soon becomes indignantly silent and leaves the soul stupefied to pursue its course of disobedience.

3. It is often seared by an individual's resorting to sophistry to justify any course of disobedience.

4. It becomes seared by breaking resolutions. When you allow yourself to break over or violate a resolution to do your duty, you have done much to sear and stifle your conscience.

5. When you violate your promise on any subject you have done much to sear your conscience. If you persist in this violation your conscience will become seared with a hot iron.

6. Conscience becomes seared by diverting the attention of the mind from the moral character of your own actions. If you suffer yourself to pass along without attending to the moral quality of your actions, your conscience will soon become seared with a hot iron.

7. Indulgence in known sin of any kind will greatly and rapidly sear your conscience.

8. Especially indulgence in presumptuous sins or those sins already put under the condemning sentence of conscience. Whenever conscience

has called your attention to the sinfulness of any act or course of action and you still persist in it, this is a presumptuous sin, and such a course will soon cause your conscience to become seared with a hot iron.

9. By indulgence in that, the lawfulness of which is regarded as doubtful by you. In speaking on the subject of meats offered to idols, the Apostle says "he that doubteth is damned (or condemned) if he eat," manifestly recognizing the principle that whatever is of doubtful lawfulness, is to be omitted on pain of condemnation, and if persisted in, the conscience will soon become seared. Thus, many persons indulge in things, the lawfulness of which they at first doubt; but directly their conscience becomes so seared that they no longer think with any degree of uneasiness whether it is doubtful or not, and they come to have no doubts about it, simply because their conscience has become seared with a hot iron.

10. By hypocritical professions conscience becomes seared—by insincere professions of friendship, or by any insincerity whatever, the conscience will soon become so seared that it can be practiced without remorse.

11. By holding on to hope already, and perhaps often, pronounced hypocritical by the decisions of conscience, it will be seared, and the hope, perhaps, grow firmer and firmer. Less and less doubt will be entertained of its genuineness in proportion as the conscience becomes seared.

12. By indulging the appetites and passions conscience becomes seared. When persons allow themselves to eat too much, at improper seasons, and improper kinds of food, merely to gratify their appetites, their conscience will soon become so seared, that they can indulge in such things without compunction. They can then go on and break down their health, and even destroy their lives by these indulgences, and then stupidly and madly ascribe their broken-down health and premature death to a mysterious providence.

13. By indulging evil tempers, pride, vanity, envy, jealousy, ambition, prejudice, hatred, whatever unholy temper is indulged, will soon so sear the conscience as to leave the mind in a state of great apathy in regard to its moral character.

14. By indulging evil habits of any kind, using tobacco in any form, or intoxicating drinks, indulging in solitary sins or secret wickedness of any kind, the conscience becomes seared in an awful and alarming

manner. How often do we find persons who can indulge in the use of tobacco, and sometimes even ministers of the gospel, can indulge themselves in that filthy abomination without remorse?

15. Conscience is seared by evil speaking. When you allow yourselves to speak unnecessarily of a brother's faults, or even uncharitably to speak of the wickedest man on earth, you do much to sear your conscience and blunt your moral sensibilities.

16. By self-justifying excuses conscience becomes seared. Whenever you resort to any form of excuse for sin, you not only harden your heart but sear your conscience, until by and by you may come into such a state as to be in a great measure satisfied with your own excuses, and fatally deceive your own soul.

17. By procrastinating the performance of duty. Whenever you defer the performance of present duty or decline or neglect to attend to that now which ought to be done at the present time, you sear your own conscience.

18. By attempts to defend error conscience becomes seared. How often men have begun only to attempt the defense of that which they knew to be error, and have ended in believing their own lie to the destruction of their souls. It is a fearful thing to attempt to defend error on any subject, and very few courses are more certain to result in a seared conscience, a hard heart and a ruined soul than this.

19. By watching for the halting of others, the conscience becomes seared. How many men by giving up their attention to the sins of others, have overlooked their own sins until their conscience has become seared with a hot iron. In this state of mind, they can see enough to blame in others, but very little in themselves. They can become censorious and denunciatory, and wonder at the long-suffering of God in sparing others in the midst of their awful iniquity, almost insensible of the fact that they themselves are among the greatest sinners out of hell.

20. By neglecting to administer reproof to those whose sins are known to us. The conscience soon becomes so seared that we can indulge in the same things ourselves with very little compunction.

21. By resenting or resisting reproof when admonished by others, by calling it censoriousness and denunciation, caviling at the manner and spirit of reproof, instead of exclaiming with David when reproved by Nathan—"I have sinned against the Lord." This is one of the ways in

which I have observed that ministers are exceedingly apt to sear their own conscience. You may have observed that they are particularly apt, at least some of them to resist and resent reproof, and sear their own conscience in a most alarming manner, while they are not ashamed to manifest a spirit under reproof which they would not hesitate severely to rebuke in anybody else.

22. By mocking God in prayer and in other devotional duties. This also is one of the ways in which church officers, and especially ministers of the gospel, are exceedingly in danger of searing their conscience. If they suffer their religious exercises to become professional rather than strictly devotional, if they suffer themselves to pray and preach and exhort because it is their business, when their hearts are not deeply imbued with the spirit of devotion, then conscience soon becomes so seared that they are ripe for ecclesiastical denunciation, excision, opposition to revivals, and almost every species of reform. How often and how distressingly has this been manifest. And what is worse than all, the conscience becomes so seared, that for these things they will not suffer reproof if faithfully administered and with the utmost kindness, without manifesting great indignation and perhaps a spirit of revenge. O, with what pain do I say this of some of the ministers of the everlasting gospel.

23. By grieving and resisting the Holy Spirit many sear their conscience. Many persons stifle and quench conviction until they have very little more moral sensibility than a beast.

24. Again by neglecting and refusing to act up to light as fast as received.

25. By neglecting to reach after light on every question of duty.

26. By neglecting universal reformation. If reformation be not universal, it cannot truly go forward at all. "Whosoever shall keep the whole law and yet offend in one point he is guilty of all." The indulgence of any form of sin renders all obedience for the time being impossible. It is a state of mind the direct opposite of holiness. If in anything therefore you neglect reformation, if you do not extend it universally over the whole field of moral obligation, your conscience will soon become seared with a hot iron.

27. By transacting business on worldly principles. No man can adopt the common business maxims of the world, and act upon them with a clear conscience. The law of God requires you to love your neighbor as

yourself. Who then can adopt the principle of making the best bargain possible, consulting only self-interest, without deeply and rapidly searing his conscience?

28. By engaging in party politics. By this I do not say that all attention to politics will sear the conscience. For as human governments are necessary, politics are to be a part of every man's religion. But mark what I say. No man can go with a party as a party, vote for the candidates and support the measures of a party, without proper regard to the moral character of the candidates and measures, without rapidly and deeply searing his conscience. How many young converts have rapidly and ruinously backslidden by engaging in party politics and by transacting business upon worldly principles. Why it is as certain as that your soul lives, if you do these things your conscience will become seared with a hot iron.

29. By exaggeration or putting a false coloring upon facts related by you, or a hypocritical covering up of the real truth, where truth ought to be known, conscience becomes seared.

30. By dishonesty in small matters, taking trifling advantage in weights and measures, little negligences in the transaction of business for others, coming late to labor, squandering scraps of time, by standing still or other inattention to business when in the employment of others, and by thousands of nameless little dishonesties, the conscience becomes deeply and ruinously seared.

31. By speaking evil of others, by receiving much good at the hand of others without any endeavor to repay them or do them good. I might pursue this part of the subject to any length, but must break off here.

VI. The Consequences *of a* Seared Conscience:

1. A certain delusion in regard to your character and deserts. If your conscience becomes so seared as not to call your particular attention to the moral quality of your actions, you are already under a deep and damning delusion in regard to your real character before God.

2. A false security, arising out of a delusion in respect to your real deserts.

3. A false hope may be, and probably will be another result of a seared conscience. If your conscience is seared, you will almost of course mistake

a mere Antinomian religion for the true religion, and hold on to a hope that is but as a spider's web.

4. A false peace, or mistaking a mere apathy on moral subjects and in respect to the moral quality of your actions, for that peace which they have who love the law of God.

5. An abandonment by the Spirit of God. Indeed, the very fact that your conscience is seared, is an evidence that the Spirit has forsaken you. And when your conscience becomes seared, it may prevent his return for ever.

6. You may be given up to the buffetings of Satan, until he may bewilder, harass, and deceive you; till he has led you to destroy your own life.

7. You may be given up to believe a lie, that you may be damned.

8. False anticipations in regard to your future usefulness. If your conscience has become seared, you may rest assured, you will do little or no good in the world. And as a general truth, you will be useless, in proportion as your conscience is seared.

9. Another consequence may be, a broken-down constitution. If you have, and will have no conscience in regard to your physiological and dietetic habits; if you will neglect or resist the light, and even sneer at these reforms, you may expect, sooner or later, to experience at least the penalty of violated physical law, in a broken down constitution, and a premature grave.

10. Another consequence may be, a worse than useless life. Do but persist in your dietetic errors, trample down the laws of your being, and madly presume upon the strength of your constitution, until you become a dyspeptic, or until some form of chronic disease has seized upon you, and ten to one if your life is not worse than useless in the world. In such circumstances, you may be so hardened, and your conscience so seared, as not to be ashamed to complain of your ill-health, and think yourself abused, if you do not have the sympathy and assiduous attention of all around you. But mark what I say. In such cases, God as deeply abhors the diseased state of your body, as if you had those forms of disease that are universally known to be a consequence of vile indulgences. If you had one of those diseases, you would expect contempt, rather than pity and sympathy. And how is it, that your conscience is so seared with a hot iron, that you can have any other form of disease, which is the result of

a reckless violation of physical law, without shame and deep remorse? For myself, I cannot be sick, unless I have been placed in such circumstances as necessarily to overwork my organs, without feeling the deepest shame and remorse. All sickness is the result of violated physical law; and when that violation can be avoided, that is a deep sin and shame, that produces sickness. But all this you may overlook, and will overlook, if your conscience becomes seared. And you may go down to your grave and to hell, under the deep abhorrence of God, for your reckless violations of the laws of your being; pitying yourself, and ascribing both your disease and death to a mysterious providence.

11. If you sear your conscience, your influence will be pernicious upon all who come within its reach. If they have confidence in you, they will be emboldened to practice what they see you practice, to say, do, and neglect, what they behold in you. And thus you may become a pest and a curse to the community in which you live.

12. You may become a great annoyance to those who are around you. I would as soon have a pestilential disease in my family as a person with a seared conscience, who can violate the Sabbath by improper conversation, improper reading, a trifling and gossiping spirit, who has no conscience in respect to attending to those things that are expected of him—can say, do, and omit many things that are inconsistent with the law of love, and yet have no conscience about it. Such a person is an insufferable annoyance and a nuisance in any family.

13. If your conscience is seared, you may in all probability ruin your posterity, if you have any. Your reckless violations of the law of love will inculcate lessons upon them that will probably ruin their souls.

14. If your conscience is seared, you will entail ruin upon the country in which you dwell, just in proportion to the amount of your influence. Are you a minister, a deacon, an elder, a man or woman of leading influence—how dreadful must be your recklessness when your conscience has become seared with a hot iron. Perhaps you can use or vend intoxicating drinks; perhaps you can use or vend tobacco; perhaps you can encourage the Church and community in the use of tea and coffee, and other worse than useless articles of luxury, and have no conscience about it—you can listen to the appeals and wails of six hundred millions of heathen, and complain of hard times, and yet have no conscience on the subject. Perhaps in a great measure through your example, the

Church and the community of which you are a member are expending vastly more, merely to gratify their appetites, and indulge their lusts, than to save a world from eternal hell, and you have no conscience about it. "*O shame, where is thy blush?*" *O man, where is your conscience?*

15. If your conscience becomes seared you will certainly do much to depress the standard of holiness, to resist the principles of reform, and hinder the conversion of the world. You will be right in the way, and yet perhaps the last man to be sensible of it. You will be a real and terrible curse to the world, and yet imagine that you are in a good degree useful.

16. If your conscience becomes seared, you may, as Achan did, bring the curse of God upon the community to which you belong.

17. If you are impenitent sinners, if your conscience becomes seared, it will effectually prevent your conversion.

18. If you have ever been converted, and your conscience becomes seared, it will effectually prevent your sanctification.

19. If it becomes seared, it may lead you into a deep delusion in respect to the degree in which you are sanctified, and you may vainly imagine, that you live without sin, while you are in the gall of bitterness and bond of iniquity.

20. If your conscience becomes seared, you will feel very little horror at the idea of sinning against God. With a seared conscience, you can expect to sin, more or less, as a thing of course, from day to day, without feeling such abhorrence of sin as to make you avoid it as you would avoid the gates of death. Nay, if your conscience becomes seared, you may plead for sin, defend it as something unavoidable, which nobody is expected to live without; and may wallow in your iniquities with very little more remorse than a swine.

REMARKS

1. From this subject we see why many persons have no conscience on a great variety of moral questions. Few things are more common, than to find even professors of religion, when expostulated with about certain habits and practices, which are as manifestly sinful, when viewed in the light of God's law, as anything whatever, reply, that they have no conscientious scruples, and indeed that they have no conscience upon the subject. They can practice many forms of intemperance, trifle with their health, squander their time and money, neglect to save, and do much to injure the world, in many ways, and yet have no conscience about it.

2. Their having no conscience on such questions, is no proof that they are not guilty in the sight of God, and that their practices are not contrary to the law of God. Their consciences are seared, and, for the time being, maintain an indignant silence. But does this prove, that what they are doing is not displeasing to God?

3. A silent or a seared conscience is a conclusive evidence that you are wrong. Conscience is never silent with respect to what is right, and will always smile its approbation, and fill the mind with peace, when you do right. When, therefore, you have no conscience at all, upon a subject—when you are not impressed with a sense of doing either morally right or wrong—when you are neither filled with peace nor stung with remorse, you may rest assured that you are wrong, and that conscience is maintaining an indignant silence.

4. A professor of religion with a seared conscience is more injurious to the cause of religion than many infidels. Who professes to look to an infidel as an example on moral subjects? But let a professor of religion have a seared conscience, and make no scruple to practice any form of intemperance, trifle with the Sabbath, become excited in party politics, transact business upon selfish principles, engage in novel reading, squander his money upon his lusts, throw away his time, speak evil of his neighbors, or indulge in any form of sin, and his example is a thrust at the very vitals of religion. Why, he is a professor of religion! It is therefore taken for granted, that almost anything he may do is right, or that to say

the least it is not inconsistent with salvation. And thus, multitudes are emboldened in sin.

5. You see that many persons mistake a seared for an approving conscience. They profess to be conscientious in what they are doing, evidently meaning by this that they feel no compunction in doing as they do, while it is manifest that they have not the peace of God, the deep approbation of conscience in the course they are pursuing. Now the absence of the approving smiles of conscience should teach them, that they are laboring under a delusion in supposing themselves to act in accordance with the dictates of conscience.

6. You see from this subject how it is that many professors of religion manage to retain their hope, notwithstanding they are as manifestly in their selfishness and sin, as they are in the world. The fact is, that their conscience has become seared with a hot iron. And having very little sense of moral obligation, they pass along securely with a lie in their right hand. To them the words of the prophet apply with great emphasis: "A deceived heart hath turned them aside so that they cannot deliver their soul, nor say, have I not a lie in my right hand?"

7. There are many persons whose consciences are seared on almost all moral subjects, and seem to have been so for a long time. They seldom or never appear to be impressed with the deep conviction that they deserve the damnation of hell. Others seem to have a conscience measurably awake on some subjects, but profoundly asleep upon other subjects, where they have for a long time resisted truth and indulged in sin.

8. It is easy to see why persons become Universalists, and reject the idea that sin deserves eternal punishment. I doubt whether there was ever a case, since the world began, in which a man became a Universalist until his conscience became seared. Nay, I doubt whether it is naturally possible for a man, with a thoroughly developed and active conscience, to doubt the justice of eternal punishment.

9. You see the importance of cultivating, especially in children, a quick, sound, thorough conscience. Their reason should be developed as early as possible, so as to give conscience, at the earliest possible hour, an influence over their will, before their habits of indulging the flesh have become too much confirmed to render it hardly possible for them to be converted.

10. You see why there is so much indulging the flesh among professors of religion, without remorse, notwithstanding they are expressly commanded to "put on Christ, and make no provision for the flesh, to fulfill the lusts thereof." Yet, as a general thing, I cannot perceive that they are not just as eager in their inquiries and efforts to obtain those things that will gratify their appetites, as most of the ungodly are. They are as great epicures, seem to take as much pains, and are at as much expense to gratify their tastes, and seem to lay as much stress upon mere gustatory enjoyment, as if to gratify their appetites is the end for which they live. Many of them will manifest as much uneasiness, and even disgust and loathing, at a plain, simple, wholesome diet, as ungodly sinners do. And yet, they appear to have no conscience on the subject. And farther, they can, not only gratify their appetite for food or drink, but their hearts seem set upon gratifying all their animal appetites and passions; and instead of "keeping their bodies under, and bringing them into subjection," they seem to have given up the rein to appetite. An Apostle might say of them, "Their god is their belly, they glory in their shame, and mind earthly things."

11. You see why so many can allow themselves to be ignorant on so many important practical questions, without remorse. Why they never have examined many questions of great moment that have often been pressed upon their attention, and when the means of knowledge are within their reach, and yet have no conscience about them.

12. When the conscience becomes seared upon one subject, it will in all probability become seared upon other subjects. And by a natural process, it will ultimately become generally seared, and prepare the way for embracing Universalism and infidelity. I might easily explain the philosophy of this, but have already said so much in this discourse that, at present, I must defer the explanation.

13. You see the infinite importance of a quick and searching conscience. It is wholly indispensable to growth in grace. There can be no such thing as a healthy piety without it.

14. But especially is a quick and searching conscience important to a gospel minister. If his conscience is seared, many sins will be practiced by himself, and suffered to exist among his people, without his reproving or even seeing them.

15. This subject shows why so many forms of sin are suffered to exist in some churches; so much selfishness, worldly-mindedness, pride, vanity, luxury, speculation, novel reading, party going, evil speaking, and many forms of sin, are allowed to exist from year to year, without rebuke, and without hardly appearing to be perceived by the minister. Now who does not see, that such a minister is "a blind leader of the blind?" His conscience is so seared, that he has very little moral sensibility. If his conscience were awake, such a state of things would wring his heart with insupportable anguish. He could not hold his peace. He would cry out in his pangs. His soul would be in travail day and night. He would lift up his voice like a trumpet, and rebuke those iniquities, come on him what would.

16. You can see the grand secret of the barrenness of many ministers. Having a seared conscience, they know not how to bring the Church under conviction for their sins. They do not know how to develop the conscience, either of saints or sinners. They know not how to enter into the secret workings of the human heart, and ferret out the various forms of iniquity that are lurking there. They do not know how to carry the light of the law of God into every department of human action, and so to develop conscience as to send a thrill of agony along every fiber of the moral nature, while indulging in any form of sin. The fact is, that if a man would get at the conscience of others, he must have a conscience himself. And again, I say, a minister with a seared conscience is "a blind leader of the blind."

17. Let this subject be a warning to young men who are in a course of preparation for the gospel ministry. My dear brethren, I beseech you to remember, that your consciences need to be cultivated as much as your intellect. And do remember, that a thorough preparation for the ministry implies, the education of the whole man. And unless your moral powers be developed, your conscience quickened, and kept in a state of intense sensibility, however great your intellectual progress may be, you can never make a useful minister.

18. We see from this subject, why so few young men do, as a matter of fact, make thorough, efficient and successful ministers. Why, in how many forms of sin do they habitually indulge, while in college, and indeed through all their course of education. While they are disciplining their intellect and acquiring a knowledge of the sciences, they are benumbing

and searing their consciences. They are, as it were, putting out the eyes of their minds, on moral subjects. In short, they are doing just what will effectually disqualify them for, and render it impossible that they should ever make successful ministers. My dear young brethren, if in your education, you indulge any form of sin; if you do not as assiduously cultivate a tender conscience, as you pursue any branch of education whatever, you not only entirely overlook what constitutes a thorough course of preparation, but, on the contrary, are taking a course that is a mere burlesque upon the idea of a thorough preparation for the ministry.

19. We see that it is utterly in vain to talk so loud and boastingly about a thorough course of training for the ministry, while so much sin is allowed among the young men in the course of training, and so little pains are taken to develop and quicken their consciences and sanctify their hearts. As a matter of fact, the present courses of education for the ministry are, to a great extent, a failure. It is in vain to deny this. It is worse than in vain—it is arrant wickedness, to deny it. "Facts are stubborn things." And the average rate of ministerial usefulness, throughout the whole of Christendom, affords a demonstration of this truth, that ought to alarm and agonize the Church, and cause those of us who are engaged in educating ministers to tremble, and inquire upon our knees before the blessed God, what it is that makes so great a majority of the young men who are trained under those influences so nearly useless in the Church of God. Will this be called censoriousness? It is the solemn truth. I say it with pain and agony; but say it I must, and say it I would, if I knew it would cost me my life. Why, beloved brethren, unless there is more conscience in the Christian ministry—a broader, deeper, more efficient, and practical knowledge of the claims of the law of God—a deeper, quicker, more agonizing insight into the depths of iniquity of the human heart—a greater abhorrence of every form of sin—a more insupportable agony in view of its existence in every form and in every degree—the world and the Church too, will sink down to hell, under our administration. I appeal to you, my brethren, who are already in the ministry; I appeal to your churches; I appeal to the lookers on; I appeal to angels and to God, and inquire, how many forms of sin are allowed to exist in you, and in your churches, without anything like that pointed rebuke which the nature of the case demands? Why, my brethren, do not many of you satisfy yourselves simply with preaching against sin, while

you are afraid so much as to name the different forms of sin that exist among those to whom you are preaching? Do you not preach against sin in the abstract, with very little or no descending to particulars? Do you arraign selfishness in all the various forms that it exists among your people? Do you rebuke their pride, self-indulgence, vanity, luxury, speculations, party spirit; and, indeed, my brethren, do you name and bring the law and gospel of God fully to bear upon the various forms of iniquity, in the detail, that exist among your people? Or are the consciences of some of you so seared, as to render you almost blind to anything like the details of sin as they exist around you? Said a discerning man in my hearing, not long since, Our minister preaches against sin; but he does not tell what sin is. He preaches against sin in general; but never against any particular sin. He denounces it in the aggregate; but never meddles with it in the detail, as it exists among his people. I do not give the words, but the substance of his remarks. Now, my beloved brethren, of how many of us could such a testimony as this be borne with truth? And how many such ministers, think you, would it require to convert the world? Of what use is it, I pray you, to preach against sin, or in favor of holiness, in the abstract, without so far entering into the detail as to possess our people of the true idea of what sin and holiness are?

20. You see the importance of praying continually for a quick, and tender, and powerful conscience.

21. You see the importance of great watchfulness, lest we should abuse and seduce our conscience, by indulgence in sin.

22. You see the great importance of faithful dealing with the consciences of all around us, so as to keep our own and their consciences fully awake, and as quick and sensitive as the apple of the eye.

23. You see the importance of self-examination, in regard to the real state of our consciences, whether they are fully awake to the whole circle of moral duties and obligations, or whether they are asleep and seared, on a great many questions that come within the cognizance of the law of God.

24. You see one grand design of preaching the gospel. It is to develop and quicken conscience, until it gains the ascendancy in the mind, and exercises that influence over the will that belongs to it.

25. You see why converts backslide, so soon after a revival of religion. It is because so little pains are taken, to quicken, develop, and keep their

consciences awake on every subject. If they are allowed to practice any iniquity; if they are not urged up continually to a full and complete renunciation of every form of sin; if they are not urged to aim at holiness, and expect to get away from all sin, they will assuredly indulge in various forms of sin. Their consciences will become more and more seared, until they can shamelessly backslide and disgrace the cause of Christ.

26. You can see what infinite evil has resulted to the Church, and is still resulting, from the denial that men are expected to live without sin in this life. Why, this denial is to my mind one of the most death-dealing errors that can be held up before the eyes of sinners. What! are men to be generally taught that they are not to expect, and even that it is a dangerous heresy to expect to live, even for a single day, without going into rebellion against Almighty God? Are they thus to be taught to expect to sin? Who does not see, that this must result in their indulging in sin, with very little remorse or self-abhorrence?

27. You see how the doctrine of sanctification in this life appears to one who has a quick and sensitive conscience. Only let a man's conscience become so thoroughly awake as that the thought of sinning is to him as terrible as death, so that conscience will roll a wave of unutterable pain across his mind, and weigh him down with agony, at every step he takes in sin—let his conscience be in such a state as to agonize his soul to a degree that will cause the perspiration to pour out from his body almost in streams, as is sometimes the case, and then present to that soul the offer of a full salvation. Tell him, if he will confess his sins, "Christ is faithful and just to forgive his sins, and cleanse him from all unrighteousness"—announce to him the fact, that the gospel has provided a salvation from sin in this life, and he will perhaps answer you at first, 'This is too good news to be true—O that it were true!' But turn the subject over, and present the scripture promises, and with what eagerness he will grasp at them. O, he will cry out, 'this is indeed a gospel suited to the circumstances and character of man. This is a salvation worthy of the Son of God.'

28. You see how this doctrine can be doubted by the church without absolute horror. Why, beloved, suppose a man's conscience thoroughly awake, until sin should appear to him in a great measure as it does to the inhabitants of heaven. Then announce to that soul that he must expect to live in sin as long as life lasts—he must expect to sin against God every

day till he dies. Why, methinks, he would shriek, and scream, and faint, and die with agony. "O horrible," he would exclaim, "with such a conscience as this, inflicting on me the pangs of the second death every time I sin, must I continue to sin as long as I live? Is there no hope that I shall escape? Has the gospel made no provision for my entire sanctification in this life? Then woe is me! I am undone. And if it is heresy to believe I shall escape from my sin before I die, O that death would come upon me this moment." This has been the actual feeling of many whose consciences have become thoroughly awake, and who were taught that there was no such provision in the gospel as that they might reasonably expect a present deliverance from all sin. Indeed, the denial of the attainability of a state of entire sanctification in this life, to an individual whose conscience is thoroughly quickened and full of power, would agonize him like the thrusting a poisoned dagger to his heart. It seems to me that within the last two or three years, I have sometimes felt as if I could not live if I did not believe the doctrine of a full salvation from sin in this life.

29. We see what the spiritual state of those must be who manifest an unwillingness to have this doctrine true. There are those who manifest the greatest want of candor in weighing the evidences in its favor, and seem disposed to resort to any shift to disprove it. It was easy to show that their writings and their sayings have every mark of an utter unwillingness to have this doctrine true. Now I ask what must their spiritual state be? What is the state of their conscience? How much do they sympathize with the inhabitants of heaven in regard to the exceeding sinfulness of sin? Do they feel horror-stricken at the idea of sinning against God? Do they know what it is to have the perspiration flow like rain when they fall into the slightest sin? Are they crying out in their prayers for a deliverance? No, but they are denouncing those that do, and who are reaching after and expecting a full salvation, as heretics and fanatics, and as explaining away the law of God!

30. You see that until the conscience of the church is quickened, but little can be done for the salvation of the world. See that tobacco-chewing minister, see that whiskey or cider drinking deacon. Why, how many forms of luxury and self-indulgence are allowed in thc Church without any conscience, while the world is going down to hell. Even agents of tract, missionary and other societies for the spread of the gospel, will go

through the country, smoking and chewing tobacco, drinking tea and coffee, and thus by their example encouraging the Church in the use of these pernicious articles, and in spending more, and perhaps ten times as much, every year for these pernicious luxuries, as they give for the spread of the blessed gospel.

31. It is amazing that tobacco-chewing ministers can (as they have in some instances, as I have been informed,) find fault with others for letting down the claims of the law. They seem at the same breath to find fault with others, for insisting upon physiological and dietetic reform, and indeed, for pressing the subject of reform so extensively as they do, and yet complain that their teaching is letting down the claims of the law of God. One of the eastern papers, but a few months since, in reviewing one of my sermons, protested in the most earnest manner against my extending the claims of the law too far. The writer said the law of God was itself strict enough, and that he must protest against its being extended beyond its real meaning. My beloved brethren, what consistency is there in maintaining at the same time two such opposite sentiments as are often maintained upon this subject? But let me say again that until the conscience of the ministry and of the church of God is thoroughly quickened upon the subject of universal reformation, the world can never be converted.

How is it possible that ministers can waste God's money, set such an example to the church, and abuse their own bodies and souls by the habitual use of tobacco, one of the most hurtful and disgusting practices that ever disgraced mankind, without compunction of conscience, and yet complain of any body's letting down the claims of the law of God, and even go so far as to write pastoral letters against the heresy of letting down the law of God, while they have no conscience on the subject of such practices. How can men be so engaged to defend the purity, the strictness, and the honor of the law of God while in the very face of their churches and in the face of heaven, they can indulge in such things as these. I would say this, with the utmost kindness and yet faithfulness to them and to God, to the church, and to my own soul. I must say it though with unutterable grief.

32. It is strange that so many churches who are living in the habitual indulgence of so many forms of sin, can manifest so much alarm at the idea of letting down the claims of the law of God. They hardly seem to

have ever thought of practicing any self-denial, keeping their bodies under, crucifying and mortifying the flesh. Almost innumerable forms of sin are allowed to exist among them without their blushing or being at all ashamed of them. And yet they manifest a great degree of alarm lest the claims of the law should be let down, and some forms of sin allowed to escape detection, and pass without rebuke. There are many things in the present day that strongly remind one of the conduct of the scribes and Pharisees, whose fears were greatly excited on the subject of our Lord Jesus Christ's letting down the law of God. They accused him of violating the Sabbath, having a wicked spirit, and of even being possessed of the devil, and seemed to be horrified with his loose notions of the claims of the law of God. They were exceedingly zealous, and cried out with great vehemence and bitterness against his want of principle and firm adherence to the law of God. I would not on any account make any such allusions as this, or say one word unnecessarily to wound the feelings of any one. But it seems to be important at the present time to call the attention of the church to the great inconsistency of exclaiming against this letting down the law of God, while they are indulging with so little remorse in great multitudes of most manifest and even flagrant violations of the law. And while we contend for universal reformation, and obedience to the law of God, they are opposing us on the one hand for our strictness, and on the other for our looseness. Nor can they contend that our strictness extends only to some subjects of minor importance, for we do insist upon universal obedience to the law of God, in heart and life.

33. It is impossible for me to understand how persons should really be in love with the law of God, earnestly and honestly engaged in supporting it in all the length and breadth of its claims, and yet indulge in so many forms of violating it with so little compunction. Is there not, my beloved brethren, some delusion in the thing? Can any man be deeply and thoroughly honest in defending the purity and strictness of that law that says—"Thou shalt love thy neighbor as thyself," who can hold slaves, use or vend alcohol as an article of common use, and encourage the church in using tobacco and other worse than useless narcotics and filthy things, to the great injury of their health, and to the robbing of the treasury of the Lord?

34. You see the mistake of supposing that conscience will always admonish us when we do wrong. When it has become seared on any point

we may continue in that form of iniquity without experiencing the rebuke of conscience.

35. We see the danger of this belief. If you take it for granted that you are not sinning, because you are not rebuked by your conscience, you will probably sleep on until you are in the depths of hell.

36. There is no safety in stopping short of universal reformation in heart and life.

37. A generally seared conscience is a fearful evidence of a state of hopeless reprobation.

38. A mind with a seared conscience is like a tub without a bottom. Truth flows right through it, and there is no such thing as influencing the will by truth. You may as well expect to influence a mere brute by moral considerations as a man whose conscience is asleep, or seared.

39. You see why so many can ridicule many important branches of reform, and even scoff at them.

40. You see why many persons cry out upon many branches of reform as legal, as self-righteousness, as something which overlooks the gospel. Here it is of the utmost importance to remember, that to do anything from a mere constrained compliance with the demands of conscience without a love to what is right for its own sake, is by no means obedience to the law of God. Conscience enforces moral obligation and love complies with it. Conscience decrees oughtness, or that you ought to do thus and thus, and benevolence walks up, joyfully and instantly, to meet the imposed responsibility. It should never be forgotten or overlooked that love is the substance of all obedience to the law of God, and that whenever the dictates of conscience are outwardly complied with for other than disinterestedly benevolent reasons, this is in reality regarding neither the demand of conscience nor of God; for conscience demands that right shall be done, and done from love to God and love to right. Whatever is not of love is not obedience to God. But again, I must say, that love or benevolence, without a most strict regard to the injunctions of conscience, is a downright absurdity. Benevolence, without universal obedience, is absurd. If there is love, there will be a most punctilious wakefulness to every affirmation of conscience. And I do not hesitate to say, that he who can call this a legal, instead of a gospel righteousness, is an Antinomian. He is guilty of a fundamental and soul-destroying error.

41. Conscience will not always remain silent. A man may in this life pervert and silence his conscience, and even destroy his moral agency, by making himself a lunatic. But let it be understood, that the time is coming when God will secure the fixed attention of the mind to those great moral truths that will arouse and arm the conscience with a thousand scorpions. When it awakes in eternity, its rebukes will be terrible beyond all description and imagination. How often it awakes even here towards the close of life, and inflicts the sharpest and most unutterable pangs upon subjects where it has long been silent. Cases have occurred under my own observation in which conscience has been so quickened upon some subjects, on which it had been nearly entirely silent, as to pierce the soul with such agonies as were almost entirely insupportable. Instances have occurred where persons have fallen like dead men, under the rebukes of conscience. In some cases, men who have been the most hardened, whose consciences have been for years seared with a hot iron, have been made to wail out, even in this life, like a soul in the prison of despair. O, sinner, O, professor of religion, do not suppose that you can always, through time and eternity, stupefy and benumb your conscience, and drown the clamors of your outraged moral nature. It will, by and by, speak out with terror and in a voice of thunder. It will sit and gnaw upon your soul and prove itself to be "the worm that never dies." It will transfix your soul as with the arrow of eternal death.

www.ingramcontent.com/pod-product-compliance
Lightning Source LLC
Chambersburg PA
CBHW020447030426
42337CB00014B/1437